I dedicate this book to my daughter Lenora R. de Abreu who inspired me to create this copy, to enjoy memorable moments with you.
Daddy loves you.

Gilsinei P. Abreu
2024

This Book Belongs to:

www.ingramcontent.com/pod-product-compliance
Lightning Source LLC
Chambersburg PA
CBHW081218260726
48653CB00010BB/3675